RED HOT CHILI GROWER

Red Hot Chili Grower

Author: Kay Maguire

First published in Great Britain in 2015 by Mitchell Beazley, an imprint of

Octopus Publishing Group Ltd, Carmelite House

50 Victoria Embankment

London EC4Y 0DZ

www.octopusbooks.co.uk   www.octopusbooksusa.com

Distributed in the US by

Hachette Book Group

1290 Avenue of the Americas

4th and 5th Floors

New York, NY 10020

Distributed in Canada by

Canadian Manda Group

664 Annette St.

Toronto, Ontario, Canada M6S 2C8

ISBN: 978 1 78472 102 2

Set in Amatic, Gill Sans, Madurai and Rockwell

Printed and bound in China

Mitchell Beazley Publisher: Alison Starling

Conceived, designed and produced by

Quid Publishing

Level 4 Sheridan House

Hove BN3 1DD

England

Cover design: Clare Barber

Designer: Clare Barber

Illustrations: Melvyn Evans

Consultant editor: Simon Maughan

RED HOT
CHILI
GROWER

The Complete Guide to Planting,
Picking, and Preserving Chillies

KAY MAGUIRE

MITCHELL

CONTENTS

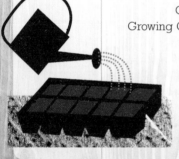

Chapter 4:
USING AND EATING CHILIS...118

FOREWORD

As garden supervisor at West Dean Gardens, West Sussex, each year I see chilis exploding into growth in one of the Victorian pit houses, bedazzling garden visitors with their vibrant array of colored fruits during summer—and I'm equally knocked out by their gorgeous diversity. I grow many edible crops, but chilis provide the "Wow!" factor, as witnessed by the annual West Dean Chilli Fiesta, which, from humble beginnings, has grown to attract about 20,000 visitors each year.

I've been growing this summer crop annually since the early 1990s, first at the request of a botanical illustration tutor at West Dean College, and afterward inspired by the tradition of chili growing in the USA, which I hoped to replicate in the UK. The collection grew from only a few different varieties of chili, as there weren't many available in UK catalogs at the time, to about 300 varieties, with nearly all of them sourced nationally—either through regular retail seed merchants or the Internet.

Chilis are a gratifyingly easy crop to grow, and relatively pest and disease free; so a thirst for heat and flavor can be satisfied easily within just one season of home-grown chili cultivation. For an experienced grower like myself, it's good to have a book with clear and positive growing tips and new ideas to embrace. Equally, using chilis with a mix of ornamentals in either pots or garden beds makes them doubly enjoyable.

However, for an absolute beginner to the world of growing chilis, some pointers on where to start are invaluable. This is where this book will prove to be a precious resource. It's a complete A–Z of chili information that will turn all who read it into paid-up members of the worldwide club of chili heads.

Sarah Wain

Garden Supervisor,
West Dean Gardens,
West Sussex, England

INTRODUCTION

From the eye-watering curries of India to the throat-tingling tacos of Mexico, chilis are one of the most widely used ingredients in the world. Every day they are included in a whole host of different cuisines, transforming any dish they're added to and, for many, chilis are an essential ingredient that they just couldn't live without.

But if you are a chili fan, have you ever thought that you could grow your very own chili supply at home? And that you don't need to be an experienced gardener to do so?

Chilis are brilliantly easy plants to grow. They need no specialist kit, just a little time, patience, and somewhere warm and bright to live. They suffer with very few problems and are impressively productive, pumping out their bright, shiny pods from mid-summer until the end of fall. Plus, with hundreds of chilis to choose from, in all different pod sizes, colors, and heat levels, there is at least one variety for you, however simple or ambitious your chili-growing plans.

Chilis are beautiful and rewarding plants, ideal for both the first-time grower and the keen gardener. For little more than the price of a packet of seeds, you could have your own favorite ingredient whenever you need it—so if you love chilis, why not give them a go?

HOW TO USE THIS BOOK

This book includes everything you ever wanted to know about chilis—from what gives the pods their heat to the best ways to grow them, both inside and out. With a helpful guide to some of the best chilis available, it is a book that can be both dipped into or read from cover to cover, depending on where your interests lie.

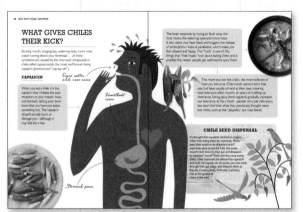

CHAPTER 1 The first chapter looks at why we love chilis so much, their history, and how they have spread across the world. It also describes why chilis are so hot and explains how this heat is measured by the Scoville Scale. Finally, the main chili species are introduced.

CHAPTER 2 covers everything you need to know to grow your own chilis. Starting with sourcing seeds and plants, it uses step-by-step instructions to guide you from seed to harvest. Symptoms of pests and diseases and how to combat them are also covered, and there are ideas and suggestions for growing chilis in different ways and in combination with other plants in the garden.

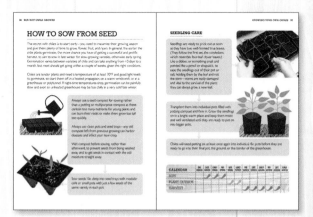

CHAPTER 3 is a clear guide to growing the many chilis available, starting with the mildest and moving up through the Scoville Scale to the superhot. It includes a range of sizes and colors, as well as varieties that are ideal for the first-time grower or for using in containers.

CHAPTER 4 covers all the many different and delicious ways chilis can be used once you have collected your harvest, whether preserving or pickling, smoking or drying. There are also a few simple but inspirational recipes.

Finally, the book ends with a glossary, explaining any technical terms, and a resources section including websites, books, seed and plant suppliers, and other general chili-related sources that you can consult if you've been bitten by the chili bug and want to know more!

Chapter 1

WHAT IS A CHILI?

Chilis are the brightly colored and often searingly hot fruit of the chili pepper plant, a group of plants known in Latin as *Capsicum* that belong to the Solanaceae family, which also includes their cousins potatoes, tomatoes, and eggplants. In culinary terms they are treated as a vegetable or spice and often called chili peppers, but they are not related to white or black pepper (*Piper* spp); the name is believed to have come from Christopher Columbus, who thought that their hot, spicy tastes were similar.

In the wild, chilis grow as perennial shrubs and hail from the tropical and temperate Americas. In cooler countries like the UK and the northern USA, they are generally grown as tender annuals. Plants vary greatly and the chili varieties available today come in all different colors, shapes, sizes, and heat strengths, with a staggering 10,000 varieties to choose from.

WHAT IS IT ABOUT CHILIS?

Chilis are the most widespread and commonly loved ingredient in the world. An essential component in the food of many countries, including India, Thailand, and Mexico, there has been an explosion of interest in this brightly colored fruit in recent years. As world cuisines fuse, people have started to realize that there is more to these little pods than just heat. Chilis are about intense flavor, too, and each country has its own unique way of cooking and using them, whether it's the sweet chili sauce of the Far East, the smoky chipotles of Mexico, or the mouth-searing curries of India.

Chilis are increasingly catching the world's attention and for many of us have become something of an obsession—people who love, grow, and eat chilis are known as "chili heads." There are contests for the biggest chili grown, the hottest chili sauce, chili challenges, and chili-eating competitions.

CHILIS ARE GOOD FOR US!

It's not all about heat—chilis are surprisingly good for us too. Valued in South America for centuries as medicinal as well as culinary plants, they are increasingly being appreciated for their many health benefits by modern medicine.

Chilis contain high levels of calcium and vitamin C—twice that of citrus fruit, with the riper red chilis having the most of all. Red chilis are also high in beta-carotene, while dried chilis are full of vitamin A. They may help to prevent diabetes, treat arthritis, ease congestion, and are claimed to boost metabolism and prevent some cancers.

Modern research also dispels the belief that spicy chilis are bad for the stomach, and it is now thought that in fact they protect the stomach lining.

RIPE RED CHILIS = beta-carotene, vitamin C, calcium

DRIED CHILIS = vitamin A

A SHORT HISTORY OF CHILIS

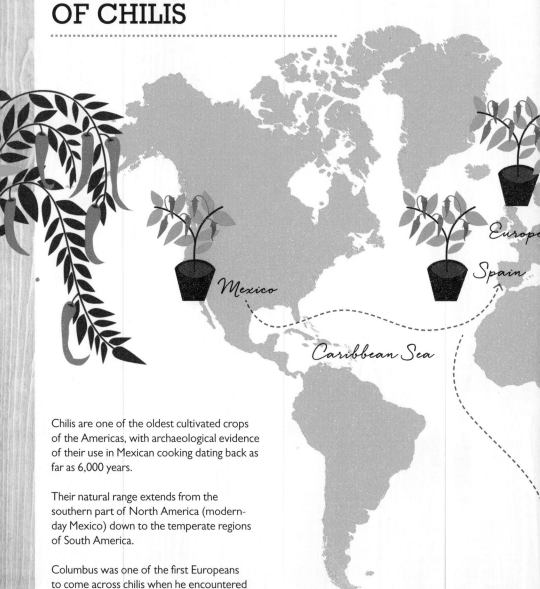

Mexico

Caribbean Sea

Spain

Europe

Chilis are one of the oldest cultivated crops of the Americas, with archaeological evidence of their use in Mexican cooking dating back as far as 6,000 years.

Their natural range extends from the southern part of North America (modern-day Mexico) down to the temperate regions of South America.

Columbus was one of the first Europeans to come across chilis when he encountered them in the Caribbean. He took them back with him to Spain.

Initially chilis were grown in Europe as botanical curiosities rather than a foodstuff but their culinary, and medicinal, potential was soon discovered. Their journey to becoming one of the most widespread and integral ingredients in the world had begun.

China

Japan

India

Indonesia

South Africa

Today India is the world's largest consumer, producer, and exporter of chilis but they are also an essential part of cuisines as diverse as Thai, Mexican, South African, Portuguese, Spanish, and Hungarian.

Spanish ships often stopped at the port of Lisbon. There is strong evidence to show that it was the Portuguese who introduced the chili to Asia, most notably to their Indian colony in Goa, as well as to China, Indonesia, and Japan.

The use of chilis then spread along the trade routes, through central Asia to Turkey and beyond.

WHAT GIVES CHILIS THEIR KICK?

Burning mouth, stinging lips, watering eyes, runny nose, sweat running down your forehead … all these symptoms are caused by the chemical compounds in chilis called capsaicinoids, the most well known being capsaicin (pronounced "cap-say-sin").

CAPSAICIN

Eyes water and nose runs

When you eat a chili it is the capsaicin that irritates the pain receptors in your mouth, nose, and stomach, letting your brain know that you have just eaten something hot. The capsaicin doesn't actually burn or damage you—although it may feel like it has.

Heartbeat rises

Stomach pain

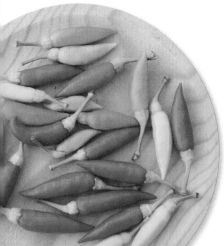

The brain responds by trying to flush away the heat, hence the watering eyes and runny nose. It also raises your heartbeat and triggers the release of endorphins—natural painkillers, which make you feel relaxed and happy. This "rush" is one of the things that "chili heads" love about eating chilis and is possibly the reason people get addicted to spicy food.

The more you eat hot chilis, the more tolerant of heat you become. Chili heads weren't born that way but have usually arrived at their awe-inspiring heat tolerance after months or years of building up resistance. Eating spicy food regularly gradually increases our tolerance to fiery food—people who eat chili every day soon find that what they previously thought were hot chilis, such as the 'Jalapeño,' are now bland!

CHILI SEED DISPERSAL

It's thought that capsaicin evolved to protect chilis from being eaten by mammals. Plants need their seeds to be dispersed and if mammals were to eat the fruit, the seeds would break down in their gut and disappear, so capsaicin "burns" them and they stop eating chilis. Only mammals are affected by capsaicin and birds can happily eat the pods, pass the seeds through their gut intact, and disperse them as they fly. Consequently, birds play a primary role in the spread of chilis in the wild.

HOW HOT?

The pungency of a chili's heat is not simply down to genetics; environmental conditions play a part, too. Stressing a plant by underwatering it can make the fruit spicier (but results in a weaker plant and therefore a poorer harvest), while the hotter the growing conditions, the more fiery a chili will be. This is particularly noticeable with fruit grown at the end of the season in fall and early winter—temperatures are low and the chilis are less hot than those grown in the summer. As a general rule, the smaller the chili, the hotter it is—but this is not always the case, so exercise caution! Chilis of the same variety can vary in heat from plant to plant, as can pods on the same plant.

THE HOT STUFF

A word of warning: Chilis can be incredibly hot. They are the key ingredient in pepper spray and some biological weapons for a reason! Capsaicin is so powerful that scientists who work with crystalline chili powder have to wear full head and body protection and work in a sealed room. High concentrations of capsaicin are toxic, and the spiciest chilis are hot enough to literally make grown men cry.

Scotch Bonnet

INSIDE THE CHILI

There is a lot of discussion about where the highest concentrations of capsaicin are found in a chili and, contrary to popular belief, it is not in the seeds but the placenta, the white pithy strip that attaches the seeds to the chili. Capsaicin spreads unevenly throughout the chili, including onto the seeds, but if you want to reduce a chili's heat you must remove all the placenta and not just the seeds. The base of the pod, called the apex, is usually the mildest part.

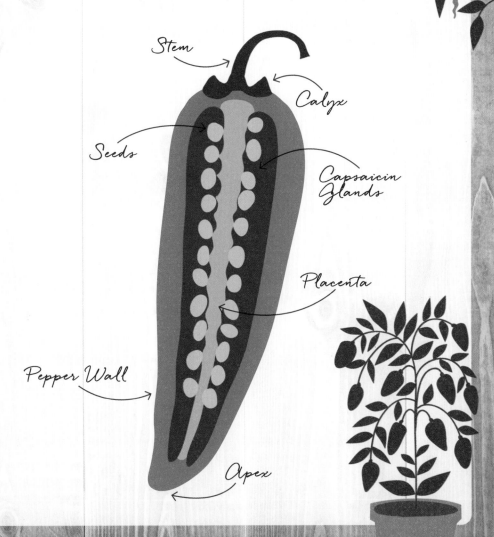

Stem

Calyx

Seeds

Capsaicin Glands

Placenta

Pepper Wall

Apex

THE SCOVILLE SCALE

Back in 1912, American chemist Wilbur Scoville developed a test for measuring the heat of chilis. He asked human tasters to sip increasingly concentrated solutions of chili diluted in a sugar syrup, until the heat of the chili could be tasted. The more the chili had to be diluted, the more intense the heat and the higher the Scoville rating. For example, if the heat was detected when the chili was diluted 300,000 times, then it was said to have a heat rating of 300,000 Scoville Heat Units (SHU).

Today, chili heat is measured with a process called high-pressure liquid chromatography, which is more scientific and reliable.

THE SCOVILLE SCALE

PURE CAPSAICIN	16,000,000
US PEPPER SPRAY	5,000,000
'SMOKIN' ED'S CAROLINA REAPER'	2,200,000
'TRINIDAD SCORPION BUTCH T'	1,463,700
'BHUT JOLOKIA'	1,000,000
'DORSET NAGA'	923,000
'SCOTCH BONNET'	100,000–325,000
'ROCOTO'	50,000–100,000
'CAYENNE'	30,000–50,000
'TABASCO'	30,000–50,000
'HUNGARIAN HOT WAX'	5,000–10,000
'JALAPEÑO'	2,500–8,000
'ANAHEIM'	500–2,500
'SANTA FE'	500–700
'PIMIENTO'	100–500
BELL PEPPER	0

THE WORLD'S HOTTEST CHILIS

1994 'RED SAVINA' 557,000 SHU,
bred and grown in California. Guinness
World Record holder.

2000 'DORSET NAGA' 1,598,227 SHU,
British bred from a Bangladeshi variety.
(Bizarrely, it was never awarded the
Guinness World Record.)

2007 'BHUT JOLOKIA' 1,000,000 SHU,
from the hills of Assam, India.
Guinness World Record holder.

2008 'TRINIDAD SCORPION' 1,200,000 SHU,
American bred.

2011 'NAGA VIPER' 1,382,000 SHU,
British bred. Guinness World Record holder.

2011 'TRINIDAD SCORPION BUTCH T' 1,463,700 SHU,
American bred from a Caribbean variety.
Guinness World Record holder.

2012 'TRINIDAD MORUGA SCORPION'
1,207,764 SHU, American bred
from a Caribbean variety.

2013 'CAROLINA REAPER'
2,200,000 SHU, bred in South
Carolina. Current Guinness World
Record holder.

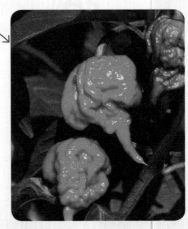

THE MAIN CHILI SPECIES

From the many native species of chilis hailing from Central and South America there are now five common domesticated chili species, and from these there are over 3,000 varieties.

CAPSICUM ANNUUM

The most widespread chili species of all, this is the main species grown in India, Mexico, China, and the East Indies. It includes sweet peppers as well as 'Cayenne', 'Pimiento', and 'Jalapeño,' and the dried spice paprika. Fruit varies in heat from zero to 80,000 SHU. Plants are usually tall and quick to germinate and fruit, making them a good choice for beginners.

CAPSICUM CHINENSE

These chilis are hot, with a fruity aromatic flavor, and are the most popular species grown in the Caribbean. They include 'Scotch Bonnet,' 'Habanero,' and 'Bhut Jolokia,' one of the hottest chilis in the world. They are slow to germinate and grow and do best in high humidity. Fruit heat ranges from a searing 100,000 to a whopping 1 million SHU.

CAPSICUM PUBESCENS

Easily identified by their black seeds and hairy leaves, these chilis are also known as 'Rocoto' and are large bushy plants capable of withstanding cooler temperatures than others. Fruit is thick and fleshy, making them unsuitable for drying. They pack a fiery 100,000 SHU.

CAPSICUM BACCATUM

Lanky plants that are happiest in the full heat of the sun, these are the most widely grown chilis in South America and are called Aji—'Aji Amarillo' is the most well known. All varieties have a distinctive smoky, fruity taste and range in heat from 3,000 to 100,000 SHU.

CAPSICUM FRUTESCENS

Small, fiery chilis. These include the famous 'Tabasco' and 'Piri Piri'. The bushy plants are great for growing in containers and for using in ornamental displays as they hold their pretty fruit upright. Grow in full sun for a tight, bushy plant. Chilis are a sizzling 50,000 to 100,000 SHU.

Chapter 2
GROWING YOUR OWN CHILIS

Chili growers can range from the novice with a couple of plants on their windowsill to the "chili head" obsessive, with greenhouses and polytunnnels bursting with colorful, fruit-laden plants. But wherever you are on the scale, most chilis are easy plants to grow, as long as they are given the right environment and a long sunny season.

Chilis can be grown from seed or bought as young plants in a variety of sizes, from very small plugs right up to almost fully grown plants. For the biggest crop they are always best grown indoors, either on a bright sunny windowsill or in a greenhouse or polytunnel. Once plants are established and the frosts have passed, chilis can also be grown outside in the garden; just make sure they are planted somewhere warm, bright, and sheltered from the wind.

GETTING STARTED

OBTAINING CHILI PLANTS OR SEEDS

Plants are available to buy from garden centers and by mail order from specialist chili nurseries from early spring onward. They can be seedlings, young plugs, or fully grown and grafted plants. These all cut out the risk of growing from seed and also help you get ahead if you don't have the room or desire to grow from seed, or missed the boat and failed to sow seed earlier in the year.

Grafted plants are pricy but more vigorous, with strong rootstocks and increased disease resistance, and they will help to guarantee a successful and heavy harvest later on in the year. They tend to come into fruit earlier and produce healthier, heavier crops and are a much more reliable choice if you have to grow outside, and a more productive one under cover. Specialist chili nurseries will always have the widest choice of plants available.

By far the best range of varieties, color, shape, and heat comes when you grow from seed. Growing from seed is also cheaper than buying plants but it will require more kit.

CHOOSING CHILIS

Growers and breeders all over the world have become quite fanatical about chilis and there are now thousands of varieties to choose from. Here are a few factors that will help you decide:

If your chilis are going outside, opt for the faster ripening, less hot varieties such as 'Padron' or 'Anaheim' so that they have time to ripen before the temperatures and light levels drop in the fall.

If you do fancy growing the hotter chilis and plan to grow them outside, make sure you have somewhere warm to continue growing them once fall arrives.

Bear in mind that *C. chinense* varieties such as 'Habenero' are more tolerant of shade, while *C. baccatum* chilis, such as 'Aji Amarillo' are more tolerant of cooler temperatures than others.

If you're planning on growing on the windowsill or in pots, look for compact varieties, many of which have been bred specifically for growing in containers, including 'Apache', 'Pot Black', 'Gusto Purple', and 'Fiesta'.

If growing in beds, borders, or pots for display in the garden, opt for the more ornamental varieties such as 'Numex Twilight.'

What kinds of chilis do you like and how do you plan to use them? Growing a range of sizes and heats will give you a choice of chilis for hot sauces, for stuffing, or for chopping through salads.

WHAT CHILIS NEED TO GROW

Chilis are easy plants to grow but to ensure a successful harvest you need to know what kind of plants they are—and therefore what they will need—before you start.

WARMTH

Chilis are tender plants, which means they cannot survive in cold weather—anything under 54°F will kill them, but they also need plenty of light and warmth for them to flower and produce fruit, and for those fruit to ripen.

Chilis need as much warmth and sun as possible. If you live in a colder climate such as the extreme north, you will get a better harvest by growing them indoors—in a greenhouse, polytunnel, or conservatory; even a small plastic greenhouse will make a difference.

When growing chilis outside, always give them your sunniest, warmest spot—a pot on a south-facing patio or in the ground at the base of a warm house wall is ideal.

TIME

In cool temperate climates, it is best to give plants as long a time as possible to grow, by starting early. Some varieties are also quicker to ripen than others—the hotter the chili, the longer it will take to ripen.

SOIL AND COMPOST

If you're sowing seed, always use seedling mix. It is finer than ordinary potting compost, which also contains too many nutrients for germination and young growth.

When potting on, give your plants good-quality potting compost. Soil-less multipurpose potting mix are perfectly good but they vary in quality and you tend to get what you pay for. They are lighter and more free-draining than soil-based composts and tend to dry out quickly and can be tricky to re-wet.

Almost all composts, unless stated, contain peat—so always check the bag before buying if you wish to avoid the potential environmental impact of this product. Never give in to the temptation to use ordinary garden soil in pots—it is likely to contain pests and diseases that will harm your crop.

WATER

Water is one of the basic needs of all plants and particularly those grown in pots, as they rely on you for their water supply.

To help you conserve water and your own valuable time, grow chilis in the biggest containers you can. Plastic pots retain water better than clay, which are more porous and dry out very quickly.

Keep compost or soil just moist at all times. Too much water will cause waterlogging, wash away nutrients, and kill the roots—and therefore the plant.

Watch plants carefully, particularly through a hot, dry summer, and once they have started to fruit, check their compost every day. If you plan to grow a lot of plants or will be away a lot, it is well worth investing in an irrigation system.

FOOD

For the very best harvest and lots of chilis, plants need feeding. Potting composts contain enough nutrients to last about six weeks, which is fine when plants are potted on regularly, but when chilis go into their final containers or the ground, always add a slow-release fertilizer to give them a boost once the compost nutrients run out.

As soon as plants start to flower, a regular high-potash feed will guarantee a bumper harvest. Chemical feeds such as tomato fertilizer are available but organic feeds such as seaweed or comfrey are also good.

WHAT YOU NEED TO GROW CHILIS

If you simply want to grow on a chili plant bought from the garden center, all you need is a sunny windowsill. Any more than that and you will need some proper kit.

PROPAGATOR

Chilis need warmth to germinate, so invest in a heated propagator or cover individual pots in plastic wrap or zip-close plastic bags to keep humidity levels up and help germination.

POTS

Use small plastic pots, or recycled yogurt containers, etc., for seed-sowing and then pot on into pots of a larger size as the plants grow. Chilis tend to grow to the size of their pot so the ideal size for most varieties—if you have the space—should be just one plant to a 2-gallon container, 12in in diameter and height. The bigger the pot you give your plant, the larger it will grow and the more prolific your harvest. Bigger pots will also prevent plants falling over when they get top-heavy with fruit.

Two smaller varieties should grow well in one growbag and very compact varieties will also grow happily in hanging baskets or windowboxes.

GROWBAG

ESSENTIAL KIT FOR GROWING CHILIS— FROM SEED TO HARVEST

POTS—small for sowing and larger ones for growing on.

COMPOST—peat-free soil-less potting mix is good, particularly in large pots.

DRAINAGE MATERIAL—terra-cotta crocks, gravel, or stones for the bottom of the final pot to enable free drainage.

STAKES AND GARDEN TWINE—to stop fruit-laden plants toppling over.

HEATED PROPAGATOR or zip-close bags, plastic wrap, etc.—aids germination.

SMALL PAINTBRUSH—for pollinating plants indoors.

WATERING CAN/HOSE—for watering plants both indoors and in the garden.

PRUNERS or sharp kitchen scissors—for pinching out, harvesting chilis, and pruning at the end of the season.

HIGH-POTASH LIQUID FEED—contains seaweed extract that supplies many essential micronutrients.

THE GROWTH CYCLE OF A CHILI

Watch your chili plant grow—from seed to leaf, from flower to fruit.

1 Seed is sown in early to mid-spring, indoors, in small 4in pots or modular seed trays.

9 Fruit is harvested (mid-summer–late fall).

8 Fruit ripens 60–120 days from sowing, depending on variety.

7 Fruit starts to appear 50 days from sowing, depending on variety.

2 Seeds germinate from within 10 days to 5 weeks, depending on variety.

3 Seedlings pricked out (see p. 37) into individual pots once they are 1in tall.

4 Chiles repotted into bigger 5in pots when roots start to appear through the holes in the base of the pot. Plants staked to prevent them leaning over as they get bigger.

5 At 12in, plants are pinched out at the top to encourage branching.

6 Flowers start to appear from 40 days after sowing.

HOW TO SOW FROM SEED

The secret with chilis is to start early—you need to maximize their growing season and give them plenty of time to grow, flower, fruit, and ripen. In general, the earlier the chili plants germinate, the more chance you have of getting a successful and prolific harvest, so aim to sow in late winter for slow-growing varieties, otherwise early spring. Germination varies between varieties of chili and can take anything from 10 days to a month, but most should get going within a couple of weeks, given the right conditions.

Chilis are tender plants and need a temperature of at least 70°F and good light levels to germinate, so start them off in a heated propagator, on a warm windowsill, or in a greenhouse or polytunnel. If night-time temperatures drop, germination can be painfully slow and even an unheated greenhouse may be too chilly in a very cold late winter.

Always use a seeding mix for sowing rather than a potting or multipurpose potting mix as these contain too many nutrients for young plants and can burn their roots or make them grow too tall too quickly.

Always use clean pots and seed trays—any old compost left from previous growing can harbor diseases and infect your new crop.

Wet potting mix before sowing, rather than afterward, to prevent seeds from being washed away and to get seeds in contact with the soil moisture straight away.

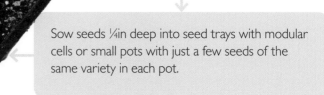

Sow seeds ¼in deep into seed trays with modular cells or small pots with just a few seeds of the same variety in each pot.

SEEDLING CARE

Seedlings are ready to prick out as soon as they have two well-formed true leaves. (They follow the first set, the cotyledons, which resemble four-leaf clover leaves.) Use a dibber, or something small and pointed like a pencil or chopstick, to ease the seedlings out of their pot or cell, holding them by the leaf and not the stem—stems are easily damaged and vital to the survival of the plant; they can always grow a new leaf.

Transplant them into individual pots filled with potting mix and firm in. Grow the seedlings on in a bright warm place and keep them moist and well ventilated until they are ready to pot on into bigger pots.

Chilis will need potting on at least once again into individual 4in pots before they are ready to go into their final pot, the ground, or the border of the greenhouse.

CALENDAR	MID WINTER	LATE WINTER	EARLY SPRING	MID SPRING	LATE SPRING	EARLY SUMMER	MID SUMMER	LATE SUMMER	EARLY AUTUMN	MID AUTUMN	LATE AUTUMN	EARLY WINTER
SOW		🌶	🌶	🌶								
PLANT OUTSIDE						🌶	🌶					
HARVEST								🌶	🌶	🌶	🌶	🌶

PLANTING OUT

Once seedlings have been pricked out and potted on into their individual 4in pots, keep growing the young plants on, keeping their compost moist. As soon as roots start to appear through the base of the pot, plant the chilis into their final container, the greenhouse bed, or ground.

PLANTING INTO THEIR FINAL POT

1 Before planting, water plants while they are still in their pots.

2 Line the base of the pot with a layer of drainage material, such as terra-cotta crocks or gravel, to ensure water can flow out of the pot easily.

3 Add potting mix to just below the depth of your chili and mix in slow-release fertilizer.

4 Remove the chili from its pot and place it on top of the potting mix. Add compost, filling in and firming as you go.

5 Leave an inch or so between the top of the pot and the compost to make watering easier and then water your plant in well.

PLANTING IN THE GROUND OR GREENHOUSE BED

1 Water the plant while still in its pot.

2 Prepare the ground before planting, forking it over to loosen the soil and break up any compacted areas and lumps.

3 Using a hand trowel, make a hole that is wider than the root ball of the chili to be planted at about the same depth.

4 Remove the pot and place the chili in the hole, making sure it is at the same depth that it was in its pot.

5 Fill in with soil, firming as you go, and water in well.

CARING FOR YOUR CHILI PLANTS

WATERING

Although chilis need regular watering and need to be checked every day in the hot, dry days of summer, do not overwater them—too much water will reduce heat intensity. Keeping them on the dry side and stressing them very slightly will help to improve flavor and produce hotter chilis but it will also produce a weaker plant and a smaller crop, so the choice is yours.

Always water plants at the base, watering the compost rather than the leaves and fruit themselves, which are more vulnerable to disease when they are wet.

If for some reason you forget to water, don't panic. A plant with the odd shriveled leaf will recover after a thorough watering. If plants have been really neglected and have got too dry, they can be revived by immersing the pot in a bucket of water until they pick up again.

FEEDING

With chilis it's all about the crop, and feeding your plants is just as important as watering. As soon as plants start to flower, begin a regular feeding regime, giving them a weekly high-potash liquid feed, which will encourage abundant flowering and fruiting. Tomato and seaweed fertilizers are popular but you can also make your own comfrey feed to help produce a large and delicious crop (see box).

STAKING

Unless you're growing a very small dwarf variety, it is a good idea to stake plants at planting to prevent them toppling over when they are laden with fruit. Place a short bamboo cane in the compost close to the plant and tie the cane to the main stem in a couple of places with garden twine. Keep tying the chili to the cane as it grows.

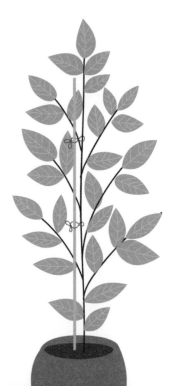

PINCHING

Once plants reach 12in, pinch out the growing point to promote branching and bushy growth farther down the plant. Simply nip out the growth buds at the tip of the main stem with your finger and thumb. It is particularly recommended for *Capsicum annuum* chilis, such as 'Jalapeño' and 'Cayenne', which have a habit of growing taller rather than wider. There is no need to prune chilis through the growing season.

COMPANION PLANTING

One last vital point—you won't get any fruit if your plants are not pollinated, ideally by visiting insects or the wind. Chilis are self-pollinating so you don't need to grow male and female plants, but to help encourage bees, butterflies, and other pollinating insects like hoverflies, grow your chilis with ornamental plants and herbs both in the greenhouse and out in the garden. Borage, lavender, marigolds, and nasturtium are all great magnets for beneficial insects, which should buzz happily around your chili flowers, pollinating as they go.

COMFREY CHILI FEED

Grow your own chili feed by cultivating a nutritious comfrey supply. Available from garden centers, comfrey grows and spreads rapidly. Look out for the *Symphytum x uplandicum* 'Bocking 14' variety, which is sterile and can't set seed and take over your garden. Once plants are established, soak chopped comfrey leaves in water in a bucket with a lid for a few weeks. The leaves will break down and the rich, dark brown liquid can be diluted 1:10 with water and fed to your plants.

GROWING ON INDOORS

You can grow plants under cover year-round. In warmer climates it is more practical to grow outside during the summer, though.

Keep an extra eye on your plants in hot weather—you may need to water every day in summer.

Open windows and glasshouse vents and doors throughout the summer to allow air to flow through the greenhouse and around the plants. This will also allow pollinating insects in.

Pollination can be tricky indoors, especially if the weather is poor. Growing companion plants such as calendula and lavender alongside chilis in a greenhouse will help. Open windows, doors, and vents as often as the weather permits to allow insects in, and give plants a gentle shake when they come into flower to help disperse the pollen.

If you want to make doubly sure, give plants a helping hand by pollinating the flowers yourself, rubbing the inside of each flower with a small brush or cotton swab. If you're planning to save the seed, wash the brush between pollinating different types of chilis to avoid cross-pollination.

In very hot weather, raising humidity will help to prevent problems like red spider mite. Regularly mist plants grown indoors or group them together on trays filled with pebbles and topped up with water. In the greenhouse, use a hose or watering can to damp down the paths and floor a couple of times a day.

If temperatures get very hot indoors, move plants outside, but harden them off for a few days first.

As the summer heat builds up, shade the conservatory or greenhouse with sheets, blinds, or white paint.

GROWING ON
IN THE GARDEN

If you plan to grow chilis outside, wait until at least late spring when all frosts have passed and then start to harden them off before they go outside permanently.

Acclimatize plants to the cooler temperatures outdoors over a period of 7–10 days by placing them outside during the day and bringing them back inside overnight. This will help them gradually get used to the change in temperature and different conditions outside.

When you finally plant them out, do it in the morning if you can to give them the whole day to settle in before temperatures drop in the evening.

Give chilis your warmest, sunniest spot, well out of the way of high winds, which can cause flowers to drop—the base of a warm, sheltered wall is perfect.

Thinking ahead and warming the soil with black polythene or cloches a couple of weeks before planting will also help to get them settled outside, as will covering them with cloches or horticultural fleece for a further two weeks after planting. Anything you can do to give them the best chance to acclimatize to the cooler outdoor temperatures will go toward helping your harvest.

As temperatures and light levels start to drop in early fall, bring outdoor-grown chilis inside (either bring the pots in or dig up and repot) where they will continue to fruit well into late fall.

HARVESTING

If they were planted early, chilis should be ready to harvest from mid-summer and reach their cropping peak by late summer, carrying on through the fall. To extend the harvest of plants that are growing outside, bring them indoors in early fall and they will continue to fruit until the light levels start to drop at the end of the season. Although they come in a range of colors, most chilis start off green and then ripen to red, yellow, purple, and even black. They can be eaten at any stage, but their flavor changes as they ripen. When chilis are green they tend to be slightly bitter and as they ripen through yellow, orange, and red, their flavor gets sweeter. Green chilis are also the hottest; red chilis are riper, and their sweetness tempers the heat, making them less fierce. When you pick a chili is down to personal preference.

HARVESTING TIPS

Harvesting the first fruit encourages the plant to produce more, so pick the first few chilis when they are still green so as to stimulate more fruit, and then from early fall leave the rest to ripen to red on the plant.

It is helpful to know the variety of chili you are growing, so that you know what color the fruit is when it is ripe and when to pick it.

If you prefer red chilis, ripen those that have been picked too early by placing them on a sunny windowsill for a few days—but remember, the longer you leave them, the drier they will become.

HOW TO HARVEST CHILIS

The riper a chili, the easier it is to pick. The first green chilis can simply be snipped off with secateurs or scissors, removing them stalk and all, as close to the stem as possible. Once they are ripe, gently pull and twist the chili off at the stem with your fingers, taking care to hold the main stem so it doesn't snap.

SAVING SEED

Although seed is relatively cheap, you could save yourself money every year—and have a bit of fun—by collecting and saving your own seed. Once you've successfully given it a go, you could get involved in seed swaps with other chili growers and extend your chili range further, for free!

HOME-COLLECTED SEEDS

Results from home-collected seed are not always as predictable as they would be with storebought—seed collected from F1 hybrids is notoriously unreliable and it is a gamble to know what sort of crop you'll get, if any.

However, seeds from most of the species of chilis are reliable as long as they haven't been cross-pollinated, by insects or the wind, with any of the other chili species you might be growing.

HOW TO SAVE SEED

If you plan to save chili seed and want it to have the same characteristics as its parent plant, do the following:

- Make sure it is not an F1 hybrid.
- Isolate the plant from other chili plants to prevent cross-pollination.
- Wait until pods are fully mature before harvesting seed—green chilis will not contain ripe seed.

- Only harvest from healthy plants.
- Remove the seeds and place them in a layer on a piece of paper towel. Pat dry and check for any damaged seed.
- Leave to dry somewhere warm, such as an airing cupboard, for a couple of weeks.
- Store in paper envelopes somewhere cool, dark, and dry, and label and date clearly—all chili seeds look the same!
- On average, chili seeds will last a couple of years.

OVERWINTERING

Although chilis are tender and will die in the winter when the temperatures get too cold, they are perennial plants and, if brought indoors, will fall dormant and can be overwintered ready for growing on again early the following spring. Not only will this give you a head start over any plants grown from seed but chilis flower and fruit even more prolifically as they mature, ensuring an even better harvest next year.

Overwintering is particularly good for the hotter, slower growing and ripening varieties such as 'Habanero' and 'Tabasco'. *C. annuum* varieties are the trickiest to overwinter.

PREPARING FOR WINTER

1 Get plants ready for winter when the temperature starts to drop in the middle of fall.

2 Choose only the strongest, healthiest plants to overwinter.

3 Move plants to a heated greenhouse or warm sunny windowsill and remove any remaining chilis—unripe fruit can be ripened off the plant.

4 Cut back branches to about 2in. This may seem drastic but it prevents the plant wasting already limited energy on leaves and branches over the winter.

5 Repot the plants into fresh new compost and water only when necessary, keeping the compost just moist.

6 As soon as the plants start back into growth in the spring, give them a high-nitrogen feed to encourage plenty of fresh new growth.

PROBLEMS

On the whole, chilis are easy plants to grow, but you may still come across problems, particularly when growing plants in the confined space of a greenhouse. However, give yourself the best possible start by growing strong healthy plants in the first place and they will be far less vulnerable to pest and disease attack.

KEEPING PLANTS HEALTHY

Always give plants the space they need. Don't overcrowd them in the border, leaving around 16in between plants, and only grow one plant per pot.

Keep on top of watering and feeding but don't overdo it—too much can cause weak, waterlogged plants.

Be aware of the problems and take steps to prevent them in the first place.

FLOWER DROP

A reasonably common problem, this is when flowers fall off the plant and no fruit develops. All plants lose a few flowers and some, such as 'Bhut Jolokia', more than others, but if it keeps happening and is affecting your harvest it might be down to a number of factors. If you're growing indoors, keep doors and vents open to allow pollinating insects in and pollinate plants yourself to make doubly sure. Leaving chilis on the plant will inhibit the production of further fruit, so keep on top of picking ripe fruit. Take care not to overwater an overwintering plant. If the weather allows, reduce watering to a couple of times a week. Chilis like stable conditions, so make sure your plants are not exposed to cold night-time temperatures or sizzling heat during the day. Keep an eye on the weather and close doors at night or use shading during the day.

LEAF DROP

If the lower leaves are falling off, it may mean you are overwatering your plants so hold back, keeping the compost just moist. Upper leaves may drop if there is a drop in temperature, plants have suffered a shock such as being potted on, or plants lack nutrients, particularly if leaves have yellow markings.

CORKING

Some types of chili, particularly 'Jalapeño,' have fine lines of pale brown scarring on the fruit when they are mature. It is nothing to worry about and just means the chili is ripe and ready to pick, even if it's green.

SMALL, MISSHAPEN, AND SEEDLESS FRUIT

This is the result of poor pollination. Follow the tips in the "Growing On" and "Growing Indoors" sections to ensure your plants are successfully pollinated.

DISEASES AND DISORDERS

DAMPING OFF

One of the first problems you may encounter, damping off is a disease that attacks seedlings and can wipe out whole trays of newly germinated seeds almost overnight. Caused by several soil-borne fungi, it is a particular problem for seeds sown early, under glass, when humidity is high and air circulation is poor.

Symptoms include collapsed seedlings, often with white fungal growth or seeds failing to germinate at all.

Always sow seed in new, clean pots and trays and fresh compost, and don't sow seed too thickly in order to avoid overcrowding. Water with tap water and ensure seeds are well ventilated.

GRAY MOLD

Gray mold, or *Botrytis cinerea*, is a common problem in crops grown under glass where conditions are very humid. It causes a gray fuzzy mold to appear on fruit as well as flowers, leaves, and stems, and commonly starts with a brown spot. There is no cure, but swift removal of infected areas can help, as can removing the plant from the greenhouse to prevent it spreading to the rest of your plants.

- Be vigilant so you can spot infections early.
- Make hygiene a priority and always clear away dead and dying leaves and flowers rather than leaving them lying around in the greenhouse.
- Reduce humidity by ventilating the greenhouse, taking care not to overwater—and always water the compost rather than the whole plant.
- Don't overcrowd plants.

POWDERY MILDEW

A white mold that appears on the upper and lower surface of the leaves, powdery mildew is the curse of dry weather and is worse where there is poor air circulation around plants—so don't overplant your chilis. Consistent watering will also help to avoid mildew.

VIRUS

Viruses are spread either by infected insects such as aphids or by contaminated hands or tools. They can cause a range of symptoms but the most common are stunted growth, distorted and yellowing leaves, damaged fruit, wilting, and sometimes death. Look for resistant varieties, always use clean tools, wash hands with hot soapy water after handling infected plants, and remove infected plants as soon as they are spotted.

BACTERIAL SPOT

Common in the greenhouse, bacterial spot causes light brown patches on the leaves, which will eventually turn yellow and fall off. It is spread in water and loves damp humid conditions, so take care when watering to water only the base of plants, keep the greenhouse clean and tidy, and don't overcrowd plants.

BLOSSOM END ROT

Dark blotches at the base of the fruit are more common on sweet bell peppers and the larger, fleshier chilis, but can be frustrating when you are so close to harvesting a long-awaited crop. Caused by a lack of calcium, blossom end rot usually occurs when erratic watering prevents the flow of calcium through the plant. More common in plants grown in pots, it can also occur when humidity is very high. Affected chilis cannot be saved but it is possible to prevent it in the first place— always water regularly and evenly and don't let the potting mix dry out.

PESTS

SLUGS AND SNAILS

These will be your biggest enemy when growing chilis outside but slugs and snails love chilis wherever they are grown, so be vigilant. The best defence is to try everything you can to prevent them. Slug pellets with ferric phosphate are advertised as less harmful to children, pets, and wildlife and are effective. Slugs also love beer, and beer traps—jelly jars sunk in the ground and filled with beer—are an easy way to catch them. Slugs and snails are mainly nocturnal and collecting on mild, damp nights always achieves good results. Dispose of slugs and snails by putting them in the trash, dissolving them in salty water, or, the more grisly method, snipping slugs in half with secateurs.

APHIDS

Aphids include both greenfly and blackfly and, although they won't usually kill your plants directly, they love soft new growth and can be prolific at the shoot tips in late spring and all through the summer. Aphids suck the sap from the leaves and can spread viruses, but also leave behind a sticky substance called honeydew, which attracts black sooty mold and makes plants look unattractive and distorted.

Aphids can be rubbed off by hand or gently hosed off; if necessary, organic pesticides can also be used. Ladybugs, lacewing larvae, and some hoverfly larvae are also their natural predators, so encourage these into the garden by planting and growing flowering plants such as marigolds, lavender, borage, and nasturtium nearby.

GLASSHOUSE WHITEFLY

Whitefly are tiny sap-sucking insects, easily spotted in the greenhouse, particularly if you brush against plants—clouds of them will fly up from your plants.

Glasshouse whitefly love the warm environment of the greenhouse, so are not usually a problem for chilis grown outside, but they will survive all year round indoors if the conditions are right.

Like aphids, they won't usually kill your plants but they will reduce vigor, making plants vulnerable to other problems, and also excrete a sticky substance called honeydew, which itself attracts ugly, black sooty mold.

Yellow sticky sheets hung in the greenhouse will trap the adult flies and some pesticide sprays can help keep them in check, but one of the best ways to control them is with biological control, which involves introducing the whiteflies' natural enemies into the growing environment.

Available from garden centers or by mail order, each biological control is specific to a particular pest; for glasshouse whitefly, it is a tiny parasitic wasp called *Encarsia formosa* that attacks and kills whitefly nymphs. It is supplied on cards that are hung on plants. It must be used before whitefly populations get too out of hand and cannot be used in conjunction with chemical sprays, as these will kill the wasps as well as the whitefly.

GLASSHOUSE RED SPIDER MITE

Common in the greenhouse but also in the garden in hot dry summers, red spider mite is a sap-sucking mite that attacks plant leaves and in severe cases can kill plants. Symptoms include yellow mottling of the leaves, leaf fall, and fine webbing strung between leaves and plants. The red spider mite loves the warm, dry conditions in greenhouses and can be a problem from spring into summer.

Increasing the humidity in the greenhouse can reduce the speed at which the mite reproduces, so always keep humidity levels up by damping down the floors every day in hot weather.

Remove infected plants straight away and wash them to remove as much of the webbing as possible. Improve the humidity and water the plants. Clear and clean the greenhouse thoroughly before reintroducing the plants to stop reinfection the following year.

A predatory mite, *Phytoseiulus persimilis*, can also be introduced in greenhouses and provides good control.

OTHER OCCASIONAL PESTS

CATERPILLARS of various moths can sometimes be found feeding on the leaves of chili plants and these can be removed by hand—a night-time search is a good way to find them if you suspect they are a problem.

CAPSID BUGS will cause distorted foliage but by the time you notice the damage, it is too late to take control measures. Fortunately, they are unlikely to affect the crop.

MEALYBUG is another sap-sucking glasshouse pest. It covers itself in a white waxy material and is usually found in inaccessible parts of the plant, such as where the branches meet the stem. They produce honeydew, which can lead to sooty mold, and they are a difficult pest to control. Organic sprays may keep them in check but they are unlikely to eliminate them. A predatory ladybug, *Cryptolaemus montrouzieri*, can also be introduced into the greenhouse.

ORNAMENTAL CHILI GROWING

A chili laden with fruit is a beautiful-looking plant and the more ornamental varieties are increasingly used as features in borders and containers, both in gardens at home and in public parks and displays.

A few chilis, such as 'Medusa' with its finger-thin chilis in red, yellow, and green, have been bred specifically for ornamental use, producing masses of stunning-looking chilis with little or no heat—not worth bothering with in the kitchen. They are perfect for bringing a flash of color and some head-turning interest, just like any other annual bedding plant such as petunias or pelargoniums.

It is also tempting, however, to use some of the more colorful-looking chilis traditionally grown for eating, such as 'Numex Twilight' or 'Poinsettia'. Fantastic dripping with fruit, remember that the more you pick, the more chilis you will get.
It might feel counterproductive but you'll need to keep picking for the display to continue.

THE BEST
DECORATIVE CHILIS

'NUMEX TWILIGHT' Dark foliage contrasts beautifully with the rainbow-colored fruit, which ripens from purple to yellow, orange, and then red—and all of these colors can be seen on the plant at the same time. Great in pots on a sunny patio. 30,000–50,000 SHUs.

'POINSETTIA' Long, thin chilis grow in upright bunches and mature from green to various shades of brilliant red. Its name comes from its resemblance to the Christmas houseplant. Large plants, so either grow in the ground or in large pots. 40,000 SHUs.

'ETNA' Smothered in bunches of scarlet chilis, this Italian bred chili is seriously hot and great in decorative pots. 65,000 SHUs.

'PAPER LANTERN' A beautiful variety with masses of large, crinkled peppers that ripen from green to vivid red. Happy in pots or as features in a bright summer border, it is also extremely hot at 450,000 SHUs!

'NUMEX PINATA' Plump, multicolored 'Jalapeño' chilis start off bright green and slowly change to yellow, orange, and then red. Easy to grow in pots. 45,000–50,000 SHUs.

'POT BLACK' A stunning black chili with dark purple leaves, purple flowers, and pods that start off black and gradually ripen to red. Tall and bushy, it makes a perfect central feature when grown with other plants in a large container. 45,000 SHUs.

GROWING CHILIS IN THE BORDER AND CONTAINERS

With their bright fruit and lush, glossy leaves, chilis are perfect for bringing a touch of the tropics to the garden and, whether they're edible varieties or not, work brilliantly in combination with other plants.

Add them to a hot sunny border once frosts have passed and they are the perfect companion to late summer perennials such as golden rudbeckias, rich red monardas, and sunny heleniums, as well as more tender plants like dahlias, cannas, and cosmos.

POT 1

The simple combination of a scarlet chili in a warm terra-cotta pot works beautifully, reminiscent of classic Mediterranean pelargoniums, and repeating the look with several pots, each with a different chili, up steps or either side of a door or gateway makes a real design statement.

POT 2

When growing chilis in containers with other plants, use as big a pot as you can and don't overplant in order to give everything room and get the best out of your plants. Remember to keep watering and feeding, particularly through the height of summer. Pick out the color of the brighter pods with annuals such as the cigar plant, *Cuphea ignea*, gazanias, and tagetes, and soften the edges of the container with trailing plants such as *Bidens ferulifolia*, dragonwing begonias, nasturtiums, and lantanas.

POT 3

Darker chilis like 'Pot Black' and 'Peruvian Purple' work beautifully with more dramatic, broody plants like amaranth (*Amaranthus caudatus*), black scabious, and the rich leaf colors of coleus, as well as lighter dusky diascias and lipstick-pink zinnias.

POT 4

Just because you're going to eat something doesn't mean it can't look great, and chilis can also be grown in pots with other edibles. For a touch of the East, grow them with scallions, bok choy, and cut-and-come-again leaves such as mizuna and mibuna.

SALSA HANGING BASKET

Eye-catching chili varieties such as 'Prairie Fire' or 'Thai Mound' are small and compact enough for growing in containers and will grow quite happily in hanging baskets—perfect if you are running out of room. Grow them together with scallions and cilantro and you've got all the delicious ingredients for a fresh salsa in one go!

Growing at eye level makes a real statement, plus they're at a handy height for picking. And don't think that these small chilis can't pack a punch—they really make up for size when it comes to flavor and just one plant will keep you in spicy chilis all summer long.

YOU WILL NEED:
- Large hanging basket
- Coir or sisal liner
- Circle of plastic cut from an old compost bag
- Potting mix
- Compact chili such as 'Prairie Fire' or 'Thai Mound'
- Scallion 'White Lisbon' seeds
- Cilantro seeds

PLANTING THE BASKET

1 Sit the basket in a pot to keep it steady and place the liner inside, making sure it is flush with the edges. Line the bottom with the plastic and fill it two-thirds full with potting mix.

2 Plant the chili in the center of the basket at the same depth it was in its pot and fill in with potting mix, firming as you go—leave a gap between the top of the basket and the compost to make watering easier.

3 Water the compost. Around the edge of the basket, make alternate sowings of cilantro and scallions and cover with a thin topping of soil.

4 Thin out the seedlings once they are big enough to handle to give them room to grow, and keep watering the basket.

5 As soon as flowers start to appear on the chili, give your plant a feed with liquid tomato fertilizer every couple of weeks. Water regularly so the compost stays moist.

6 Start picking as soon as your crops are ready and remember that the more chilis you pick, the more you will get.

Chapter 3

CHILI
SELECTOR

There are literally hundreds of different chili varieties, ranging from the very mild to the tear-jerking record breakers. There is a chili out there for everyone—be it the foodie, the first-time grower, or the chili head. Chilis can be grown inside on the windowsill or outdoors to bring a splash of color to the garden. Wherever you wish to grow them and however you want to use them, there is a whole host of delicious, lively varieties to choose from.

It is not possible to include every chili here but a selection of the most popular, flavorful, ornamental, and easy to grow has been chosen. They are listed in heat order, from the very mild to the superhot.

Capsicum annuum
'ANAHEIM'

ORIGIN: Although originating in New Mexico, 'Anaheim' was brought to Anaheim, California, and given its name.

APPEARANCE: Large, cone-shaped chilis 6–8in long and 1in wide. Fruit is shiny and mature from a deep green to red, but is most often used when green.

HEAT LEVELS: Mild (500–2,500 SHU).

SOWING: Quick-growing chilis, sow 'Anaheim' no later than early spring in a warm, bright place.

GROWING: 'Anaheim' chilis are known as a New Mexican pod type, a group of chilis developed at the New Mexico State University. Plants are upright but quite lanky, reaching 24–30in in height, and need support to prevent them toppling over when covered with fruit. They do not overwinter as well as other chilis. Fruit is ready to pick about 80 days from sowing.

COOKING AND EATING: Mild but sweetly flavored, 'Anaheim' are large, with a thick skin and an open cavity, making them perfect for stuffing. Mainly used when green and mild, they are often the key ingredient in chili verde, a traditional Mexican stew, and chili rellenos— chilis stuffed and battered, then fried. They also freeze and dry well, and are great chilis for bringing a little heat when eaten fresh.

Popular in Mexican cuisine, 'Anaheim' make the perfect stuffed chili.

Capsicum chinense
'ROCOTILLO'

ORIGIN: *C. chinense* 'Rocotillo' is the most common chili grown in the West Indies and the island of Puerto Rico.

APPEARANCE: Almost round, 'Rocotillo' chilis are squat, wrinkled little peppers, similar in shape to their cousins the 'Scotch Bonnet.' Pods ripen from green to red and hang from a very long stem.

HEAT LEVELS: Mild (1,000–2,000 SHU).

SOWING: Ensure these slow-growing plants have time to fruit and ripen by sowing early, by the end of winter at the latest.

GROWING: 'Rocotillo' are bushy but tall plants reaching 35–47in high. Like all *C. chinense* peppers, they are slow-growing; despite their mild heat, pods take a long time—up to 150 days—to ripen to maturity from seed.

COOKING AND EATING: These small chilis have a mild but fruity flavor. Their thin flesh dries well and is good for slicing in salsas or fried with other vegetables. They are also a popular ingredient in Spanish soups and stews.

Not to be confused with the rocotillo chili, a similar but C. baccatum Type from Peru.

Capsicum annuum
'ANCHO POBLANO'

ORIGIN: Puebla, Mexico. In Mexico, they are known as 'Poblano' when fresh, and 'Anchos' when dried.

APPEARANCE: Large, wide, heart-shaped fruit, growing up to 5–6in long. Immature fruit are dark green, warming up as they ripen to a red so deep that it is almost black.

HEAT LEVELS: Mild (2,000–3,000 SHU).

SOWING: Sow seed 2in deep into damp, fine seedling mix.

GROWING: Easy to grow, producing bushy plants that grow up to 3ft high—plants will need support when dripping with their large fruit, so stake when planting into their final spot. They are extremely productive, taking just 90–100 days from seed to harvest, and can be used when both a dark glossy green and deep red.

COOKING AND EATING: 'Ancho Poblano' are mildly hot, slightly sweet chilis, often harvested when green and immature. These fresh green poblano pods can be roasted and peeled and are the favored chili for stuffing and making into chili rellenos. They are also popularly left to ripen to red and then dried to make anchos, the key ingredient in the Mexican sauce "mole."

Large chilis perfect for stuffing or adding a little zing to pasta, stews, and meat dishes.

Capsicum annuum
'SANTA FE GRANDE'

ORIGIN: South America. Also known as Guero chili.

APPEARANCE: Thick, fleshy, conical-shaped chilis with pods that grow up to 3in long. Generally harvested when fruit are yellow but can be left to ripen to red.

HEAT LEVELS: Mild (2,500– 5,000 SHU).

SOWING: To avoid disturbing young seedlings, sow seed into individual pots, if you have the room, or modular trays if space is limited.

GROWING: A great chili that is easy to grow and crops early, with fruit ready to pick 80 days from sowing. 'Santa Fe Grande' are attractive plants that are well balanced and compact, with a strong single stem. They produce fruit easily and prolifically and are attractive focal plants. 'Santa Fe Grande' are resistant to tobacco mosaic virus.

COOKING AND EATING: These slightly sweet, chunky chilis are said to have a melon tang and are lovely eaten fresh in salads, sandwiches, and salsas.
They are a perfect chili for stuffing with cheese and grilling but are also good roasted, in pasta, chopped onto pizza, or pickled.

'Santa Fe Grande' are a type of wax chili—named after their shiny, waxy pods.

Capsicum annuum
'FRESNO'

ORIGIN: Fresno, California.

APPEARANCE: Dainty fruit appears upright on the plant and is small and cone-shaped, just 2in long and ¾in wide. It ripens from light green to orange to a rich red when fully mature, popping up among neat green leaves.

HEAT LEVELS: Mild (5,000 SHU).

SOWING: An easy chili to grow, sow in early spring into clean, preferably new, pots or trays.

GROWING: 'Fresno' copes well in cooler climates, growing quickly and maturing to ripe fruit in just 100 days from seed (this lessens to 80 days when grown inside). Plants are upright and sturdy, reaching only 16–20in tall, and are hugely productive—a great plant for the first-time chili grower.

COOKING AND EATING: 'Fresno' have a mild heat and delicious fresh flavor and can be eaten both green and red. They are lovely eaten whole and great in salsas and salads. In California they are popular for use in ceviche and with rice and black beans. 'Fresno' are thin-skinned chilis, perfect for pickling and freezing, but are not recommended for drying.

One of the most popular chilis grown in the USA.

Capsicum annuum
'HUNGARIAN HOT WAX'

ORIGIN: South America.

APPEARANCE: Long, thin pointed fruit that can grow up to 4in in length. Chilis mature from pale green to yellow, orange, and finally crimson if left to ripen on the plant, and become hotter as they age.

HEAT LEVELS: Mild–medium (2,000–8,000 SHU).

SOWING: Sow undercover in modules in late winter to early spring.

GROWING: A brilliantly quick and early-fruiting variety that is ripe and ready for picking about 80 days from sowing. Ideal for cooler climates, 'Hungarian Hot Wax' will sometimes fruit very early, which can stunt its growth—if this happens, simply nip off the first fruit to give the plant time to develop further.

COOKING AND EATING: 'Hungarian Hot Wax' chilis are perfect sliced into salads and stir-fries, barbecued, fried, or broiled whole and stuffed with goat's cheese and herbs.

This variety can be turned into pickles or savory jam if you have a glut.

Capsicum annuum
'CHERRY BOMB' F1

ORIGIN: South America.

APPEARANCE: A brilliant-looking chili, bright red and almost 2in round.

HEAT LEVELS: Mild (2,500–6,000 SHU).

SOWING: Sow seed under cover into modules or pots in late winter or early spring.

GROWING: 'Cherry Bomb' are easy to grow and produce sturdy plants that reach heights of 24in. They are heavy croppers and quick to produce their mild, chunky chilis, which are ready to crop 80 days from sowing. As an F1 hybrid, this chili will not come true from seed.

COOKING AND EATING: Thick-skinned chilis, 'Cherry Bomb' are full of flavor but pack just a gentle punch. They make great salsa, but are also delicious stuffed or roasted, and make excellent pickle. They can be eaten both green and red.

One of the best chilis for growing outside in colder climates, ripening well in even the dullest summers.

Capsicum annuum
'PIMIENTOS DE PADRON'

ORIGIN: Mexico, although they are named after the area in Galicia, Spain, where they were first cultivated.

APPEARANCE: These small, perfectly conical chilis will grow up to 4in long and are slightly crinkled, with a subtle groove down the side. They range from bright green to red as they mature.

HEAT LEVELS: Mild–medium (0–12,000 SHU).

SOWING: An easy chili to grow; sow indoors no later than early spring.

GROWING: Plants are large and bushy, growing to 6ft when grown in the ground, and will crop continuously, provided you keep on picking. They grow and crop well outside and are ready to harvest as green fruit 100 days from seed.

COOKING AND EATING: 'Padron' are traditionally picked when they are immature and green, about 2in long and before they have developed any heat. However, although the majority are mild and sweet, the odd few can be very hot indeed, depending on how much warmth and sunlight the pods received while they were growing. It is impossible to tell whether a chili is hot or not other than by eating it, making eating a dish of 'Padron' a culinary game of Russian roulette!

A traditional Spanish tapas dish, fried whole in olive oil with a sprinkling of sea salt.

Capsicum annuum
'JALAPEÑO'

ORIGIN: Xalapa, Veracruz, Mexico. Pronounced "halapeno," the chili is named after the town where it was traditionally grown.

APPEARANCE: Stocky, green, bullet-shaped fruit 2–4in long.

HEAT LEVELS: Mild–medium (2,500–10,000 SHU).

SOWING: Sow indoors in late winter to late spring. Sow ⅓in deep in trays or, alternatively, two seeds per pot.

Jalapeño juice is drunk as a remedy for cardiovascular problems.

GROWING: One of the world's most famous chilis, 'Jalapeño' is a popular and easy plant to grow, producing heavy harvests of crisp, green fruit. Generally harvested when green, the fruit will ripen to red if left. Plants reach a height of around 30in and fruit continuously from late summer onward, or 80 days from sowing. Other varieties include 'Purple Jalapeño.'

COOKING AND EATING: 'Jalapeño' have a distinctive flavor and a thick skin, which makes drying them tricky. They are therefore commonly either pickled or smoked—and called chipotles, which have a richer, sweeter flavor. Delicious with nachos and tacos, they are also often stuffed with cheese, seafood, or meat. They are a popular ingredient in salsas and other chili sauces, and the juice is drunk as a remedy for cardiovascular problems.

Capsicum annuum
'SERRANO'

ORIGIN: Native to the Serrano mountain range of south and central Mexico.

APPEARANCE: The finger-shaped glossy pods start off green and gradually ripen to red, brown, orange, and then yellow. Pods are small, around ¾–2in long and just ¾in wide.

HEAT LEVELS: Medium (10,000–25,000 SHU).

SOWING: Sow seed two to a pot or individually into modular trays in late winter.

GROWING: 'Serrano' are bushy, high-yielding plants that can grow to between 18–24in tall and produce up to 50 pods per plant. They take 100 days to mature from seed to fruit and are better grown indoors in a consistently warm spot than outside.

COOKING AND EATING: Often eaten raw, 'Serrano' are one of the most popular chilis in Mexican cooking. They are a popular choice for relishes and salsas such as pico de gallo, and the chunky fruit can be harvested when either green or red. They are not ideal for drying but are good pickled as well as roasted and have thin skins so there is no need to peel them.

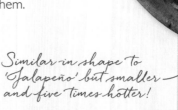

Similar in shape to 'Jalapeño' but smaller and five times hotter!

Capsicum annuum
'JOE'S LONG'

ORIGIN: Thought to have been bred in the Calabria region of Italy.

APPEARANCE: Very long, slender, cayenne-style chilis that can reach an astonishing 12in in length. Fruit is wrinkled and ripens from a dark bottle green to a bright vibrant red, often curling and twisting as it grows.

HEAT LEVELS: Hot (20,000–30,000 SHU).

SOWING: Sow seed 2in deep or place on the surface of seedling mix and cover with vermiculite.

GROWING: An easy, good-looking, and fun chili to grow, with fruit appearing within 80 days. Plants are gangly and lanky, reaching around 24in tall, and are best grown in the ground rather than a pot, although they look amazing in full fruit. They become top-heavy and in need of support when laden with fruit, so stake when planting into their final position.

COOKING AND EATING: Fruit is thin-fleshed, drying very well and therefore good for grinding into powder. It is also great in curries, hot sauces, and sliced into salads. A great-looking chili for using to spice up oil in decorative bottles and jars.

Head-turning fruit that is possibly the longest chili of all!

Capsicum annuum
'DEMON RED'

ORIGIN: South America.

APPEARANCE: Tiny, slender fruit grows to just 1in long. It matures from bright green to orange to a vibrant glossy red. Pods grow in clusters and point upward on the plant.

HEAT LEVELS: Hot (20,000–30,000 SHU).

SOWING: Fill pots, trays, or modules with seed compost, water the potting mix, and then sow seeds 2in deep.

GROWING: Plants are compact and bushy, reaching to just 14in, and are abundant fruiters. The fruit is quick to ripen to maturity, taking just 80 days. 'Demon Red' is a brilliant ornamental variety, with pretty white flowers and lots of bright, colorful fruit. They make sweet plants for a windowsill or basket.

COOKING AND EATING: A favorite in Thai cooking, these little chilis have a good kick and are great for using fresh in curries and Thai dipping sauces. The small, thin-skinned pods also dry well and make great chili flakes and powder. They are ideal for flavoring oils and using in marinades.

Neat little plants bred specifically for growing in pots, windowboxes, and hanging baskets.

Capsicum annuum
'FILIUS BLUE'

ORIGIN: South America.

APPEARANCE: Beautiful plants with neat, purple leaves, occasionally flecked with cream, and fruit that is a bright purple-blue, staying that way before finally turning yellow, orange, and then deep red. Pods are cherry-shaped and held upward on the plant. Shades of each color appear on the plant at the same time.

HEAT LEVELS: Hot (20,000–30,000 SHU).

SOWING: Sow seed in pots and trays and place somewhere warm, at a temperature of at least 70°F, until they germinate.

GROWING: Stocky, bushy plants that grow to about 24in tall and are ideal for growing in pots on the patio. These are great little chilis for growing outside, maturing well in dull summers, while their distinctively colored fruit make an interesting talking point. 'Filius Blue' are easy to grow and quick to ripen, reaching maturity within just 80 days from seed.

COOKING AND EATING: Best harvested when blue and devilishly hot, 'Filius Blue' add a colorful kick when eaten fresh in salsas, salads, and sandwiches. They also freeze well whole, straight from the plant, and can be dried and ground or flaked.

'Filius Blue' are unusual chilis that start off blue and very hot but lose their heat as they ripen to red.

Capsicum annuum
'CAYENNE'

ORIGIN: South America, but named after the Cayenne River in French Guiana. Brought by Portuguese traders to Europe, Africa, and India.

APPEARANCE: Long, slender pods that grow anywhere from 4 to 8in long. Pods mature from dark green to bright red, have wrinkled flesh, and a distinctive 'Cayenne' curl.

HEAT LEVELS: Hot (30,000–50,000 SHU).

SOWING: For a heavy harvest, sow in late winter or early spring somewhere warm and bright under cover.

GROWING: One of the best known spicy chilis, 'Cayenne' are grown commercially in Africa, India, Japan, Mexico, and some southern states of the USA. Plants are tall and bushy, reaching 24–40in in height, and make attractive feature plants in a conservatory or pots outdoors. They reach maturity after around 70 days and will fruit prolifically. Varieties include 'Long Slim Cayenne', 'Golden Cayenne', 'Long Purple', and 'Cayennetta'.

COOKING AND EATING: 'Cayenne' are popular in a wide range of cuisines and are most commonly dried and ground into cayenne pepper and used in stews and sauces. They are also great in pickles and salsas. The pretty pods have a thin wall and so dry easily, making them ideal for use in decorative wreaths and chili ristras.

The favorite chili for use in Cajun cooking and in the famous Louisiana-style hot, vinegary sauces.

Capsicum frutescens
'TABASCO'

ORIGIN: Mexico. Named after the Mexican state of Tabasco.

APPEARANCE: Small, upright fruit that changes from yellow-green to yellow, to orange, and then scarlet. Fruit is tapered and around 1½in long.

HEAT LEVELS: Hot (30,000–50,000 SHU).

SOWING: Sow seed sparingly and do not overwater, keeping the potting mix just moist.

GROWING: Attractive, bushy plants with fruit maturing at different stages and colors across the plant. 'Tabasco' reach heights of between 47–70in and are productive plants, producing up to 100 pods per plant. Plants today are usually of the Greenleaf strain, which is resistant to tobacco mosaic virus, a disease that almost wiped out crops in the 1960s. Fruit is mature approximately 100 days after sowing.

COOKING AND EATING: Mature red 'Tabasco' chilis are the key ingredient in the world-famous Tabasco sauce, which has been produced in Louisiana since 1848. 'Tabasco' have a smoky, spicy flavor and are great when used fresh in salsas, pickles, and other sauces and savory jams. They are an ideal chili for adding a punch to cooking oils. 'Tabasco' chilis are central to Creole cooking.

'Tabasco' are the only variety of chili that are juicy rather than dry inside.

Capsicum baccatum
'AJI AMARILLO'

ORIGIN: Archaeological evidence shows this chili was domesticated in ancient Peru 2,500 years ago.

APPEARANCE: Fruit is conical, wrinkled, and 4–6in long, ripening from green to a deep, warm orange. Pods turn yellow when cooked, hence their name, which translates literally to "yellow chili."

HEAT LEVELS: Hot (30,000–50,000 SHU).

SOWING: Sow indoors and place in a heated propagator or on a warm bright windowsill.

GROWING: Aji are tall, large-leaved plants with a tendency to sprawl when grown in the ground and can become small trees if given a long enough growing season. Plants reach a height of 5ft and fruit from 120 days after sowing. Other varieties include 'Aji Limon' and 'Colorado'.

COOKING AND EATING: Aji have a distinctive smoky, fruity flavor, with a hint of citrus and a searing heat. Delicious both fresh and roasted in salsas and sauces, the pods have a thin flesh so they also dry easily and make good chili powder when ground. The chili of choice for the South American seafood dish ceviche—fish marinated in lime and chili.

Aji are now the most commonly grown chili in South America.

Capsicum annuum
'NUMEX TWILIGHT'

ORIGIN: Mexico.

APPEARANCE: 'Numex Twilight' produces masses of glossy, ¾in upright fruit that changes through the rainbow colors of purple, yellow, orange, and then red. A real beauty.

HEAT LEVELS: Hot (30,000–50,000 SHU).

SOWING: Quick to ripen; sow seed in early spring into seed trays or individual pots.

GROWING: A gorgeous ornamental chili, 'Numex Twilight' are upright, compact plants reaching just 24in high. They grow well in pots and are happy outside once established, although yield may be less. Plants take 80 days from seed to fruit and overwinter well. Developed at the New Mexico State University, 'Numex Twilight' is one of the New Mexican chilis. Other varieties include 'Fairy Lights'.

COOKING AND EATING: Almost too pretty to be eaten, 'Numex Twilight' have a very respectable kick and are delicious eaten fresh, sliced into salsas, salads, and curries. The fruit is thin-walled, so freezes and dries well.

Produces fruit continuously, making plants multicolored when smothered in fruit.

Capsicum annuum
'POT BLACK'

ORIGIN: British bred.

APPEARANCE: A spectacular and dramatic-looking chili with black-tinted leaves and stems, and pretty purple flowers. The small fruit grows to ¾–1½in and is held upright on the plant. Pods are a deep, glossy black and will eventually ripen to scarlet as they mature.

HEAT LEVELS: Hot (45,000 SHU).

SOWING: Sow seed into damp seedling mix no later than early spring.

GROWING: 'Pot Black' are bushy, slightly straggly plants that are very happy in containers and are small enough to grow in a windowbox, or even a hanging basket. Plants grow to 20in high and 16in wide.

COOKING AND EATING: With a clear, intense flavor, 'Pot Black' are hot enough to pack a punch in any dish and are ideal for adding to stir-fries and curries as well as eating fresh in salads and sandwiches. Pods are best picked when black but they can also be left on the plant to mature to red. 'Pot Black' chilis dry and freeze well.

These jet-black pods make a great talking point at the dinner table.

Capsicum annuum
'PRAIRIE FIRE'

ORIGIN: South America.

APPEARANCE: Plants produce lots of small, upward-pointing fruit that change from lemon yellow, through to purple, orange, and finally red. Pods are only 1in long and ⅓in wide.

HEAT LEVELS: Hot (70,000 SHU).

SOWING: Perfect for windowsill growing, sow these compact chilis into 4in pots in a bright kitchen.

GROWING: 'Prairie Fire' are dwarf, bushy plants that reach a height of 8in and a width of 12in. They are attractive ornamental chilis, perfect for growing in pots on the patio or a sunny windowsill inside, and are a very quick, hot chili, reaching red maturity within 130 days.

COOKING AND EATING: These small, fiery chilis are very versatile and perfect for growing in the kitchen for picking as and when you need them. 'Prairie Fire' can be eaten fresh or roasted at any stage of ripeness and can be frozen or dried. They are great sliced into salads, stir-fries, and curries, as well as used in salsas or homemade chili jam.

Easy to grow 'Prairie Fire' are an ideal plant for the first-time chili grower.

Capsicum annuum
'APACHE' F1

ORIGIN: British bred.

APPEARANCE: Masses of little stubby fruit, 1in long and ⅔in wide, that matures from a light green to a bright, shiny red.

HEAT LEVELS: Hot (70,000–80,000 SHU).

SOWING: Easy plants to germinate; sow in early spring in a heated propagator or on a warm, sunny windowsill.

GROWING: A reliable grower and producer, 'Apache' are quick to fruit, taking 95 days from seed to harvest. They are dwarf, compact, sturdy plants, reaching just 12–16in high, making them ideal for container growing, which will also help to "bonsai" the plants. Simply pick the pods as and when you need them, but keep picking to encourage more pods to develop. A great variety for the first-time chili grower. Note—'Apache' are F1 hybrids, which means that seeds will not come true.

COOKING AND EATING: A versatile, everyday chili that can be used fresh in anything from salsas to chocolate cake. Pods dry well and can be ground into flakes or powder; they can also be frozen.

Just the thing for kitchen windowsills, windowboxes, and hanging baskets.

Capsicum annuum
'RING OF FIRE'

ORIGIN: South America.

APPEARANCE: Long, thin, scarlet pods, ⅓in wide and up to 3in long, that ripen from a bottle green to bright red.

HEAT LEVELS: Hot (70,000–80,000 SHU).

SOWING: Sow seed into individual pots or modular trays in late winter or early spring.

GROWING: A quick-to-ripen, hot 'Cayenne' type that can be picked when either green or red—chilis are ready to pick 100 days from sowing. 'Ring of Fire' is an attractive-looking upright bush, around 18in high and very productive, producing masses of pods continuously, just as long as they are regularly picked.

COOKING AND EATING: 'Ring of Fire' is a fiery treat eaten fresh and is great for slicing into hot dishes as well as in salads, sandwiches, and salsas. It is an ideal chili for use in hot fruity sauces and, as a thin-walled chili, it also dries very well to make flakes and good hot ground chili powder. Pods also freeze well.

A great chili for a pot on a sunny patio or in a conservatory.

Capsicum chinense
'ORANGE HABANERO'

The name 'Habanero' is often used wrongly to describe all *C. chinense* chilis, but it is a distinct single species and pod type.

ORIGIN: The Yucatan Peninsula, Mexico.

APPEARANCE: A stunning-looking chili that is stocky and lantern-shaped. Only around 1in long, it matures from green to a bright golden orange.

HEAT LEVELS: Hot–superhot (80,000–300,000 SHU).

SOWING: 'Habanero' can take a couple of weeks to germinate, so be patient.

GROWING: 'Habanero' are slow to grow and need 200 days to produce ripe pods. In cooler climates where there are not 200 frost-free days with temperatures above 70 degrees, these peppers have to be grown inside with supplemental lighting. They are bushy plants about 28in tall and wide. Today, 'Habanero' is grown commercially on the Yucatan Peninsula, Belize, Costa Rica, and the USA. Other varieties include 'Hot Chocolate Habanero,' 'White Habanero,' and 'Red Habanero.'

'Habanero' chilis are named after the Cuban capital, La Habana.

COOKING AND EATING: With a thin waxy flesh and a fruity citrus flavor, 'Habanero' chilis are often used raw in salsas and salads, as they lose some of their flavor, although not their heat, when cooked. They are often made into hot sauces and also freeze and dry well. Dried and powdered 'Habanero' has a delightful apricot scent.

Capsicum chinense
'SCOTCH BONNET'

ORIGIN: Central and South America. 'Scotch Bonnet' are now one of the most common chilis in the Caribbean and are grown extensively in Jamaica.

APPEARANCE: 'Scotch Bonnet' are distinctive, stout little chilis, globular in shape, and almost as long as they are wide. Pods change from green to yellow, to orange and then red, and are around 1½–2in long and wide.

HEAT LEVELS: Superhot (200,000–350,000 SHU).

SOWING: Get ahead with these slow-growing plants by growing on nursery or storebought plug plants. Otherwise sow seed early.

GROWING: Plants are short and bushy, reaching only 20in, and are slow to mature, with fruit taking 160 days to ripen from seed, so sow early. Other varieties include 'Scotch Bonnet Chocolate', 'Scotch Bonnet Yellow', and 'Mini Bonnet'.

COOKING AND EATING: Integral to the food of Jamaica, the Cayman Islands, and other parts of the Caribbean, 'Scotch Bonnet' provide the unique kick in "jerk" cooking, a dry spice seasoning that is rubbed onto meat such as chicken and pork and contains the principal ingredients of 'Scotch Bonnet' chili and allspice. The chilis have a sweet flavor and are best eaten fresh in sauces and salsas but can also be frozen, pickled, or added to oil.

'Scotch Bonnet' are thought to bear a resemblance to the Scottish hat, the tam-o'-shanter, hence the name.

Capsicum chinense
'PAPER LANTERN'

ORIGIN: Mexico.

APPEARANCE: Attractive pendant, teardrop-shaped fruit that grows to 2–3in long and is slightly wrinkled. The fruit appears in clusters, ripening from lime green to orange, and finally scarlet.

HEAT LEVELS: Superhot (350,000–400,000 SHU).

SOWING: Sow no later than mid-spring for a productive harvest.

GROWING: 'Paper Lantern' are tall, attractive plants with a bushy habit and look lovely in pots covered in their distinctive shaped pods. Although a habanero chili, 'Paper Lantern' is easier to grow than other habaneros—it is quicker to ripen from seed, taking a good two weeks less than others at approximately 90 days, and is therefore a more productive plant. Plants will grow well outside in a sheltered sunny spot.

COOKING AND EATING: Along with blistering heat, 'Paper Lantern' have a sweet, fruity tang and are perfect for hot sauces or barbecue marinades. They freeze well but their fruity flavor is best when the pods are fresh. Use in spicy soups, stews, and salsas.

'Paper Lantern' have a short growing season, making them great for a cooler climate.

Capsicum chinense
'DORSET NAGA'

ORIGIN: Bred in England from the 'Naga Morich,' a Bangladeshi chili bought in an Asian food store.

APPEARANCE: Fruit ripens from emerald green to a deep red and is a distinctive chili—stocky little cone-shaped pods, only 2in long, with a finely wrinkled skin.

HEAT LEVELS: One of the world's hottest chilis (500,000–1 million SHU).

SOWING: Give these superhot chilis as long a growing season as possible by sowing in mid- to late winter.

GROWING: 'Dorset Naga' are slow to germinate and grow, so are best grown indoors or in a greenhouse rather than risk a poor crop outside. They are great croppers and can produce hundreds of chilis if given a long season in the greenhouse border; pods are ready to pick about 175 days after sowing. They can be eaten as both green and red fruit.

COOKING AND EATING: Like many superhot chilis, 'Dorset Naga' is a "slow burner," which means the heat doesn't hit you straight away—always wait before taking a second bite if you're mad enough to eat one fresh! As well as extreme heat, they have a fruity flavor and scent, making them perfect for chutneys, sauces, and curries, but use sparingly—a little goes a very long way.

In the greenhouse bed, 'Dorset Naga' can reach 5ft tall, but they will be smaller when grown in pots.

Capsicum chinense
'BHUT JOLOKIA'

ORIGIN: Assam, India. Also known as Naga Jolokia, Naga Morich, and the Ghost Chili.

APPEARANCE: Unique-looking chilis, 2–3in long and 1in wide, with a bulbous shape and a fine, crumpled skin. Pods ripen from lime green to orange and then red.

HEAT LEVELS: One of the world's hottest chilis (more than 1 million SHU).

SOWING: Tricky chilis to grow, 'Bhut Jolokia' germinate erratically but presoaking seeds in chili plant food or using a heated propagator set at 86°F is said to help speed up germination. Keep seed moist but do not overwater, as it is susceptible to rotting.

One of the world's hottest chilis: use only one pod between four people.

GROWING: 'Bhut Jolokia' need a long hot season to reach maturity and produce a good crop, so are only for indoor growing and patient, dedicated growers. Plants are tall, reaching 45in, and may need staking as fruit start to swell. Flower drop is common and plants can take 175 days from seed to ripe orange pods. Other varieties include 'Bhut Jolokia White', 'Bhut Jolokia Peach', and 'Bhut Jolokia Chocolate'.

COOKING AND EATING: 'Bhut Jolokia' have a persistent heat that can last for hours after eating, but also have a fruity aroma and taste. Use very sparingly in sauces and mouth-searing curries—the very thin-fleshed pods dry well and are best ground (with care) and added in tiny amounts.

Chapter 4

USING AND EATING CHILIS

Chilis are one of the most popular ingredients on the planet and an integral element in many cuisines. They pop up in all sorts of recipes and can be used fresh, whole, sliced, dried, smoked, and ground. The possibilities are almost endless, but however they are used, chilis are guaranteed to bring added warmth and zing to any recipe.

Growing chilis can become very addictive and they are heavy-fruiting plants, so you should have more than enough fresh pods to add to any recipe; but if you end up with more chilis than you know what to do with at the end of the season, there is no need to waste your harvest—there are plenty of different ways to preserve chilis and make the most of your crop.

DRYING CHILIS

Drying is one of the oldest and most traditional ways of preserving chilis. In hot countries such as India and Mexico, heaps of them laid out in the sun to dry are a familiar sight. Drying works well for most chilis, but some definitely dry better than others, particularly the thinner-walled, less fleshy types such as 'Cayenne'. Chunky, fleshy ones like 'Jalapeño' and 'Santa Fe Grande' don't dry so well but are good smoked or pickled.

Drying outside in the hot sun is not an option for many of us but we can still have a go. The key is to put them somewhere warm and dry to slowly remove all the moisture from the pods—if any moisture is left in the chilis, they will rot.

Dried chilis are still full of concentrated oils. As they shrink when drying, they are hotter, weight for weight, than fresh pods. They also have a different taste, often becoming richer in flavor.

Thin chilis like 'Ring of Fire' can be dried on a warm sunny windowsill or laid on trays in an airing cupboard for a few days, but for large amounts and for bigger chilis there are other options.

DEHYDRATORS

A dehydrator is a good investment, particularly if you've been bitten by the chili bug and plan to preserve in the future. They are easy to use (and not just for chilis; you can dry everything from fruit to meat) and consist of stacking drying racks that are warmed by hot air from a fan. Simply lay chilis on the racks—larger varieties can be cut in half—with their seeds and pith removed, to dry slowly.

OVEN DRYING

The key with this is not to have the oven too hot or you will burn the pods rather than dry them, which at the very least will make them bitter, and at worst, unusable. Drying chilis slowly over a low heat will also help them keep some of their color.

Slice the chilis and lay them out on baking parchment spread on cookie sheets. Put them in an oven on a very low heat, 210°F or less. Leave the door ajar if you are worried about burning them and check on them after half an hour to see how they are doing. Keep checking them regularly after that—the thicker the chilis, the longer they will take. Chilis are dry when they snap apart easily but are still supple.

STORING DRIED CHILIS

Keep dried chilis in a moisture-tight container or jar in a cool, dry, dark place. They should keep for a couple of years, although they are best used within six months.

Dark spots or patches are sure signs that moisture has got in and pods should be thrown away.

Whole dried chilis can be rehydrated, crumbled into soups and sauces, or tossed whole into curries or stews.

CHILI FLAKES AND POWDER

If you've got lots of dried chilis, it's worth making them into flakes or grinding them into powder, as they take up far less room. However, once broken and powdered, chilis lose their essential flavor oils much faster than those left whole.

Put dry chilis into a food processor, breaking them up as they go in, and pulse until they are coarsely ground. Alternatively, pound them by hand in a mortar and pestle. Don't breathe in!

Chili flakes are brilliant sprinkled over roasting vegetables, rubbed into meat, or added to oil for a hot and fruity marinade.

GROUND CHILI

Dried chilis can also be ground into powder, but remember fresh powder has the best flavor so don't grind up too large a batch.

Grind in a spice mill or coffee grinder (one specifically reserved for chilis from now on is a good idea) and always wear a mask as well as goggles if you are grinding the superhot varieties. Give the lid of the grinder a knock before lifting it off to allow the powder to settle. Store in small airtight jars.

REHYDRATING DRIED CHILIS

In some Mexican and Indian dishes, whole dried chilis are rehydrated before use. Simply put them in a bowl of warm water, weigh them down with a small plate or saucer, and leave for 30 minutes. They can then be chopped into curries, stews, and salsas, blended into a paste, or stuffed.

MAKING A CHILI RISTRA

In hot parts of the world, like Turkey, India, and South America, long red garlands of chili can be seen everywhere. They look brilliant but they're also a very traditional way of preserving chilis, hanging them up to air dry in the sun for use later on.

Here is the simplest way to string chilis into ristras (as they are called in Mexico).

YOU WILL NEED:
- A large needle.
- Fine string or fishing line.
- Lots of ripe chilis, preferably thinner, quick-drying chilis such as 'Cayenne.' Use red rather than green chilis in case they don't turn red.

1 Tie a thick knot at one end of the string or line and thread the other through the needle.

2 Start threading your chilis by making a hole with the needle through the stem.

3 Keep the needle pointed up and thread the stem near the top so that the chilis fall down the string.

4 Keep arranging the chilis as they fall so that there are no gaps in your ristra.

5 When you've finished, knot your string or line at the top.

6 Hang your ristra in a warm, dry place where it will get plenty of sun, and nip out any chilis that start to rot.

MEXICAN RISTRA

The traditional, but slightly trickier, Mexican way is to tie bunches of chilis along a length of string and then to wind these around a longer, stronger loop of twine that is hung from a beam or the top of a door.

SMOKING

Smoking is a popular way of preserving the meatier chilis, particularly in Mexico, and the most famous of the smoked chilis are chipotles. Often wrongly believed to be a variety of chili in their own right, chipotles are simply chilis, and most commonly 'Jalapeños', that have been slowly dried while being flavored with smoke.

In Mexico they are traditionally smoked on racks over large pits connected by an underground tunnel to a fire in a nearby pit. You can have a go at smoking your own chilis at home, although it can take time.

A purpose-built smoker is ideal but a barbecue works just as well, and if you dry them in the oven first you can cut the whole smoking and drying process down from 24 hours to just three or four.

HOW TO SMOKE CHILIS

YOU WILL NEED:
- A kettle barbecue with a lid (either cleaned thoroughly to remove any meat residue or a new one, dedicated to smoking chilis)
- Charcoal briquettes
- Hickory, pecan, mesquite, or other mild woodchips for smoking
- Firm, ripe 'Jalapeño' chilis, either whole or cut in half to speed up the drying process

❶ Dry your chilis on trays in a very low oven (210°F) until they are dry but not stiff.

❷ While the chilis are drying, soak the woodchips in water. This will help them to burn slowly and produce plenty of smoke.

3 Pile briquettes into the middle of the barbecue and light them.

4 Once they turn gray, move them into two piles with a gap in the middle and cover them with the soaked woodchips.

5 Lay the chilis on the center of the rack above the gap rather than the coals—you don't want to cook them, just dry and smoke them.

6 Cover with the lid, leaving the vents only slightly open. This will allow in just a little air and keep the fire burning nice and slowly.

7 Check regularly, adding briquettes and chips as needed, and move the pods around to keep them away from the fire.

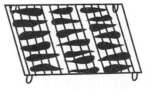

8 After 3–4 hours the chilis should be dry and will have absorbed plenty of smoke. Remove them from the barbecue and leave to cool.

Either freeze your chipotles or store them in sealed jars in a cool, dry place. As with other dried chilis, they can be rehydrated or ground into flakes or powder. Chipotles make delicious rich smoky sauces, chutneys, and marinades.

PICKLING

Pickling is a simple and traditional method of preserving that can be used with any chili type and enables you to enjoy the flavor and texture of your chilis up to a whole year from picking.

Make sure you clean and sterilize your jars first to avoid any lurking bacteria. You can do this by putting them through a hot dishwasher cycle, filling them with boiling water, and leaving them to stand for 20 minutes or washing them well and drying them in an oven at a very low temperature. Do this just before you use them to lessen the time they are sitting around, and always pour your pickles into warm jars so that they don't cool down too quickly before the seal is closed. Pickled chilis should keep for up to a year.

HOW TO PICKLE CHILIS

YOU WILL NEED:
- 6 sterilized jars
- 6 cups vinegar—wine vinegars are milder than malt and won't swamp the chili heat with the taste of vinegar. Cider vinegar has a fruitier tang
- 2 cups water
- I cup sugar
- Cooking salt—table salt tends to clump
- Fresh chilis
- Plus: bay leaves, peppercorns, garlic, onion … whatever you like, to taste

1 Mix 6 cups of vinegar with 2 cups of water and I cup of sugar in a large saucepan.

2 Bring to a boil and leave to simmer gently for a couple of minutes.

3 Pack 6 large sterilized jars with chilis and add I teaspoon of salt to each, plus a few bay leaves, peppercorns, and any garlic and other herbs you might want.

4 Top up with the vinegar and sugar mixture, filling the jar right up to the rim.

5 Give the chilis a careful stir to get rid of any air bubbles and seal with a tight lid.

PRESERVING CHILIS IN OIL

Fresh chilis cannot be preserved in oil for any length of time. They are susceptible to rotting and, more terrifyingly, bacteria, that could even lead to botulism. If you do wish to put fresh chilis in oil, they must be kept in the fridge and eaten within a couple of weeks. Dried chilis, on the other hand, keep very well in oil, flavoring it beautifully and intensifying in heat over time.

USING OIL

Simply add chili flakes and a few whole dried chilis to a pan of olive oil and heat gently for around 5 minutes. Piercing the whole chilis first will help the oil get inside them.

Decant into a sterilized bottle and seal with a lid. Give it a good shake and store in a cool, dry place for a few weeks.

Shake it every week and watch the oil slowly take on a warm red tint as the chilis infuse.

FREEZING CHILIS

Freezing is by far the easiest way to preserve chilis, and they keep their fresh taste and heat brilliantly. They don't need to be blanched beforehand—simply wash whole, healthy, ripe chilis, make sure they are thoroughly dry, and then pop them into sealed plastic bags or tubs and into the freezer.

ALTERNATIVELY:

Prepare and slice them, removing the seeds, and lay them out on trays in the freezer for a couple of hours—this will stop them sticking together. Once they are frozen, put them in bags until you are ready to use them.

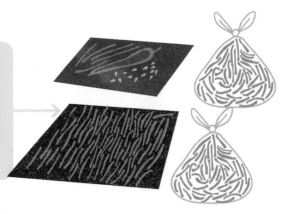

Finely slice chilis, put into ice cube trays, and top up with water. Once frozen, put the cubes into bags and use them in cooking, as required.

COOKING WITH CHILIS

Chilis are one of the most prodigiously used ingredients in the world, transforming and adding an extra dimension to everything from salads and sandwiches to soups and stews.

Below are some simple but delicious recipes to help you make the most of your crop but, before you do, remember: chilis can be unpredictable. It may be one of the things that "chili heads" love about them, but if you do get taken by surprise, water is not the answer. Capsaicin is not soluble in water so no matter how much you drink, it won't ease the pain. It is very soluble in fats and oils, however, so if you're caught out drink milk or eat plain yogurt and swill it around your mouth before spitting it out. It should take the chili heat with it. Some also swear by vegetable or sunflower oil.

A WORD OF CAUTION

If you are chopping very hot chilis, always wear gloves—the disposable latex ones are good as you can still feel what you are doing. If you don't and you rub your eyes, your mouth, or anywhere else, the pain can be excruciating.

If you're preparing and cooking with chilis, particularly if you plan to grind or dry them, it's also a good idea to wear eye protection—and a mask if you're grinding superhot ones. Don't be tempted to stick your nose over a pan of bubbling hot sauce and inhale deeply—you will regret it!

HOW TO PREPARE CHILIS

Always handle the hottest chilis by the stalk and wear gloves for extra protection.

To remove the seeds, cut the top off and roll the chili in your hand until all of the seeds fall out.

To remove the pith, or membrane, cut the chili in half and slice out the white central part. If you're careful, it is possible to do this without touching it by only holding the sides of the chili.

CHILI RECIPES

PERFECT PADRONS

This recipe couldn't be simpler and makes a quick and delicious lunch or early evening snack. Eat the chilis with your fingers, holding them by the stem—although the majority have no heat at all, the odd one is a scorcher! Serves 1.

INGREDIENTS
- 7–8 Padron peppers
- 1–2 tbsp olive oil
- sea salt

- Rinse and dry the chilis and leave them whole, with their stems intact.
- Heat the oil in a large frying pan and, once it is hot, add the chilis.
- Cook the chilis, turning them frequently until they are brown and starting to blister.
- Remove, drain on paper towel, put on a plate, and sprinkle with the sea salt. Serve warm.

SIMPLE SPICY SALSA

The perfect accompaniment to everything from salads to barbecued meat and broiled fish, salsa also makes a fresh, and aromatic dip. Serves 4 as a dip.

INGREDIENTS
- 6 ripe tomatoes
- 1 red onion, finely chopped
- 1–2 tbsp finely chopped fresh green chilis
- 2 roasted red bell peppers (from a jar is fine), finely sliced
- 1 tbsp olive oil
- 1 garlic clove, crushed
- juice of 1 lime
- bunch of cilantro, finely chopped

- Halve the tomatoes and scoop out the seeds, then chop finely.
- Put in a large bowl and add the remaining ingredients. Mix together and keep in the fridge until you're ready.

SWEET CHILI SAUCE

The classic dipping sauce for spring rolls and Thai fishcakes, but equally delicious with meat or fish kebabs, even sausages. Remove some of the membrane and seeds from the chilis if you don't want the sauce to be too throat-warming. Makes 1 standard jar (12oz).

INGREDIENTS
- 2–3 red chilis, finely chopped
- ½ cup superfine sugar
- 7 tbsp rice or white wine vinegar
- ½ cup water
- 1 garlic clove, crushed or thinly sliced

- Put all the ingredients in a pan and bring to a boil.
- Lower the heat and simmer for 30 minutes, then whizz in a blender until finely chopped—sweet chili sauce needs a little texture.
- Put the mixture in a clean pan and simmer until it's nice and sticky.
- Store in a sterilized jar in the fridge for a couple of weeks.

CHIPOTLE CHUTNEY

A gorgeous rich smoky sauce that is amazing with burgers, cold chicken, or simply bread and cheese. Makes 1 standard jar (12oz).

INGREDIENTS
- 7 tbsp vinegar
- ½ cup brown sugar
- ¼ cup superfine sugar
- 1 apple, cored and chopped
- 1 garlic clove, crushed
- 1 chipotle chili, chopped
- 3 fresh chilis, finely chopped
- ½ tbsp minced ginger
- salt, to taste

- Put all the ingredients in a pan and bring to a boil, stirring frequently.
- Lower the heat and simmer for around 45 minutes until the chutney has reduced and thickened.
- Leave it to cool and store in a sealed sterilized jar in the fridge for up to a week.

CHILI RELLENOS

This traditional Mexican snack literally translates as "stuffed chilis" and is a stuffed, roasted 'Poblano' chili, filled with either cheese or minced meat and covered with an egg batter and fried. Any larger, chunkier chili like 'Jalapeño,' 'Anaheim,' or 'Hungarian Hot Wax' will also work well. If you can't get Monterey Jack, use another cheese that melts well, such as Gruyère. Serves 4 as a starter.

INGREDIENTS
- 12 large green chilis
- 7oz Monterey Jack, grated or finely sliced
- oil, for deep frying

BATTER:
- ½ cup plain flour
- pinch of salt
- 1 large egg, separated
- ⅓ cup iced water
- 1 tbsp vegetable oil

- Roast the chilis by laying them over a bare flame, such as a gas hob, or putting them under a broiler.
- Keep turning the chilis until the skins blacken and start to blister.
- Remove them from the heat and put them in a sealed plastic bag to cool.
- Meanwhile, make the batter. Sift the flour into a large bowl and add a pinch of salt. Whisk the egg yolk and water together, then whisk into the flour with the oil to make a smooth batter. In another bowl, whisk the egg whites until stiff and then fold into the batter.
- Once the peppers are cool, the skins should slip off easily, but running them under cold water will help—wear latex gloves if you are skinning hotter chilis or your fingers will be sore.
- Slit each pepper by running a sharp knife down one side. Remove the seeds and membrane if desired.
- Stuff with the cheese. (The chilis will be softer if you used the broiling method to roast them, so be careful not to tear them while stuffing.)
- Pour about 2in of oil into a large pan or wok (you need enough to cover the chilis) and heat (high).
- Dip each chili into the batter and then drop into the oil. Deep fry, turning the chilis frequently until they are evenly brown all over.
- Drain on paper towel and serve.

CHILI CHOCOLATE BROWNIES

A spicy take on a classic, perfect for chili heads with a sweet tooth!
The combination of chocolate and chili has been popular in Mexico and South America for centuries and if you love chilis you'll love these—they are rich and warm rather than hot; just add more chili if you want more of a kick. Makes 12–18 squares.

INGREDIENTS

- 7oz semisweet chocolate, broken into chunks
- 1 cup muscovado sugar
- ¾ cup butter, plus extra for greasing the pan
- 1 mild red chili, finely chopped
- 3 eggs, separated, at room temperature
- 1¼ cups all-purpose flour
- 1 tsp chili flakes
- 3oz semisweet chocolate chips

- Heat the oven to 350°F. Grease a 9in × 9in baking pan and line with baking parchment.
- Put the chocolate, sugar, butter, and chili in a pan and heat gently, stirring constantly, until it has all melted together.
- Once the mixture has cooled, add the egg yolks and flour and beat together.
- Whisk the egg whites until they stand up in soft peaks, then add a spoonful to the chocolate mix and stir to combine.
- Fold in the remaining egg whites.
- Pour the mixture into the baking pan and sprinkle with the chili flakes and chocolate chunks.
- Bake for about 25 minutes, until evenly risen.
- Leave to cool, then cut into spicy squares.

GLOSSARY

.ANNUAL
A plant that completes its life cycle—germinating, flowering, and dying—in one year.

CAPSAICIN/CAPSAICINOIDS
The chemical compounds found in chilis that cause the burning sensation are capsaicinoids. Capsaicin is the main capsaicinoid.

CULTIVAR
Contraction of "cultivated variety," also shown as "cv." Refers to a plant that originated in cultivation rather than in the wild and is often used interchangeably with the term "variety" (or "var.").

DIBBER
A hand tool, cylindrical in shape, used to make sowing or planting holes.

DIE-BACK
The death of a stem or other part of a plant following localized damage or infection. Symptoms include wilting leaves and discolored areas, which need to be pruned out to prevent spreading.

FAMILY
A category in plant classification that groups together related genera, for example the family Solanaceae, which includes *Capsicum* and *Solanum*.

GENUS
A category in plant classification that describes a group of closely related plants ranked between family and species.

GRAFTED PLANTS
Plants that have been created by artificially joining together the rootstock of one plant and the shoot (scion) of another. Grafted plants display greater vigor and disease resistance and are often used for greenhouse border growing, where disease may be present. Popular grafted plants include chilis as well as tomatoes and eggplants.

GROWBAG
A commercial plastic bag filled with nutrient-rich potting compost that is used for growing crops rather than growing them in the ground or pots.

HARDEN OFF
To gradually acclimatize plants that have been raised indoors to the cooler conditions outside

MISTING
Spraying plants with a fine mist of water to increase the humidity in the air around them. It is often done to combat pests such as red spider mite.

PERENNIAL
A plant that lives longer than two years.

PLUG PLANTS
Plants that are bought as young seedlings or plants and grown on. An alternative to growing plants from seed.

POTTING ON
Transplanting seedlings or young plants into bigger pots to give them room to keep growing.

PRICK OUT
To transfer young seedlings from the pot or tray where they germinated into larger pots so that they have room to grow.

REPOTTING
The process of transferring a plant grown in a container into a new pot the same size, after reducing the rootball slightly to make room for fresh compost.

SPECIES
A category in plant classification, below genus, of closely related, similar plants.

TENDER
A plant that is especially vulnerable to frost damage.

VARIETY
A category in plant classification used to describe a group of closely related, naturally occurring plants that will come true from either seed or cuttings. It is ranked below species and is often used interchangeably with "cultivar."

WAX
A pod type of *Capsicum annuum* with very shiny pods, such as 'Santa Fe Grande.'

FURTHER RESOURCES

WEBSITES

The American Horticultural Society
www.ahs.org

The Chile Foundry
www.chilefoundry.com

ChiliGrower.com
www.chiligrower.com

The Chile Man
www.thechileman.org

Chile Pepper
www.chilepepper.com

The Chilli Pepper Company
www.chileseeds.co.uk

Chili Pepper Madness
www.chilipeppermadness.com

The Chile Pepper Institute
www.chilepepperinstitute.org

ChilePlants.com
www.chileplants.com

The Chile Woman
www.thechilewoman.com

The Fiery Foods and Barbecue
Supersite
www.fiery-foods.com

International Chili Society
www.chilicookoff.com

Peppers.com
www.peppers.com

Pepper Joe's
www.pepperjoe.com

Seeds of Italy
www.seedsofitaly.com

FESTIVALS AND FIESTAS

Hatch Valley Chile Festival
www.hatchchilefest.com
August. Hatch, New Mexico

Havelock Chili Festival
www.chilifestival.org
October. Havelock, North Carolina

Houston Hot Sauce Festival
www.houstonhotsauce.com
September, Houston, Texas

BOOKS

Butel, Jane, *Chili Madness: A Passionate Cookbook*. Workman Publishing Company, 2008.

DeWitt, Dave, and Bosland, Paul W., *The Complete Chile Pepper Book*. Timber Press, 2009.

DeWitt, Dave, *The Chile Pepper Encyclopedia*. William Morrow Cookbooks, 1999.

Pollock, Michael (Ed.), *Vegetable & Fruit Gardening*. DK, 2012.

Houghton, Harmon, *Red or Green Chile Bible*. Clear Light Publishing, 2014.

INDEX

IMAGE CREDITS